To all the poets who have walked before me,
to those who will come after . . .

And to the poets, friends, and family
who have taken the journey with me . . .

Thank you!

Walk on the Heart Side

LOVE POEMS
by Linda Levokove

May you always walk on the heart side.

Linda Levokove

Cedar Creek Publishing
Virginia, USA

Cover photo by Linda Levokove

Cedar Creek Publishing
Bremo Bluff, Virginia
www.cedarcreekauthors.com

Printed in the United States of America

Library of Congress Control Number 2010932982

ISBN 978-0-9842449-4-2

CONTENTS

DREAM LOVER

I slip into the familiar softness of your flesh,

close my eyes and let the darkness come,

go to that empty space where image is shaped.

You hold my hand and gather me to your heart,

I inhale the subterranean scent of your kiss.

Complete, I sleep, secure as a child, a seed . . .

a single grain of sand.

EVENSONG

Twilight's ripe stillness burns the lake,
a fiery scarf on blood-green algae

Fingers of grass fondle twisted vines,
open-eyed fish shake winter scales

Spring flicks leaf-tongues on naked trees,
paints blank blooms with color

Birds, butterflies, sated with seeds and nectar,
blissfully glide into evening

Gazing at the sky, two lovers lie,
glowing like so many stars,

waiting to kiss the night.

THE DANCE

In the sky's vast ballroom
swirling moonbeams

make slatted shadows
on ruffled raiment

luminous blossoms of light
shower golden sparks
on fields of dewed daffodil horns
lemon-yellow like suns

veiled and scattered . . .
Will your hand reach out

your lips touch my cheek
our hesitant breath meet

or will we dance on and on?

EBB AND FLOW

Daylight dallies still, spreads her last
golden glow across the darkening sea

where iridescent seashells lushly bloom,
bouquets more beautiful than white peonies

that soothe all those faded salted memories,
and once again evoke your breathless kiss,

though they will be forever imprinted
on my dry and thirsting lips.

RIPTIDE

My hungry heart

wants to run wild

free as the sea

beating . . . striving

toward nocturnal depths

riding the red tide

where a hot carnal moon

marries sand and mud

and blood thrums

an ageless surge

till only the luminance is left.

I LOOKED OUT THE WINDOW

White hills

blue cold

gray sky

naked trees

winter drowse

chimney smoke

days held

days lost

like lovers

gone

EXHALE

Each breath, evasive as a moment

evaporates yesterdays

promises no tomorrows

Waiting in an empty space

that once housed my heart,

you suck the last vapor from my mouth

and kiss my skin bloody.

I know you . . . I call you lover.

FIVE COURSE MEAL

Appetizers served –
Aromatic herbs tangoed on my tongue . . .
your hand grazed my knee.

Salad ensued –
Snakes of curly greens cooled my palette . . .
you caressed my cheek.

Soup presented –
you kissed my neck.

Entrees appeared –
Rare meaty juices wet my lips . . .
fingers tip-toed up my thigh.

Desserts paraded by –
Mountains of mousses, chocolate concoctions,
fruity tarts, and more. . . .

WE HEADED FOR THE DOOR!!

FLOWERING

Your breathe is sweet

your tongue silken as a dewed petal

each kiss is a flower

on my love bruised lips

IN THE GARDEN

We frolic through the woods
where steep and sultry grass
tease our tender feet.

My toes cool in the clear stream
where schools of golden fish
polish my skin smooth.

Gathering daisies white and gold,
wildflower bouquets, garlands
for my wind-waved hair.

Rainbow-colored butterflies flutter,
slowing to sip the moisture
from my bare dewy neck.

Alongside the fig tree, naked as a jay,
you hold a basket of succulent fruit.

Reclining at my side, you listen
to the robins sing, a choir of bees
humming a chorus fit for a king.

"Would you like a pear?" he said.

"Thanks, I'll have the apple instead."

THE CAT

Voluptuous cat

you creep into my bed,

spread your desirous claws

and pretend to worship at my feet.

In your wild amber eyes I see

the jungle's green mysteries –

but so confident are you in your charm,

your supreme serene sovereignty,

you offer me the rarest of raptures,

a hum of a purr from your orange throat.

ITALIAN HOLIDAY

The night wind shakes me awake,
outside a miasma of streetlamps,
magical reflections on the Arno.

Earlier, we walked on the bridge,
argued, you flapping your hands,
me shouting, until back in our room
we ate pasta takeout and made love
until dark shadows crept up the walls.

We slept, curled like the pale noodles
that had fallen on the terrazzo floor.

This wasn't love forever, just for now,
and reminiscent of Chinese food,
I knew we'd soon be hungry again.

JUST BREATHE

A blanket spread smooth on the beach
your arms, barrier to an unquiet sea.

Moonlight swims in the bubbles puddled
in your champagne glass.

You take pins from my hair, hold back
waves until the last star turns to ash.

Your scent rises from crumpled sheets of sand.

"Happy New Year, darling"

I think I might die . . . being loved by you.

INVITATION

Come to me, my indolent beast,

when night is deep and starless.

I long to rake my fingers

through your thick tawny mane,

lick scorched tears from empty eyes,

bury myself in hot heaving flesh,

smell the wild perfume of your sour breath,

hear the expulsion of your rattled snort.

In this soft and sumptuous pillared lair

I can banish time . . . unremember.

LANDSCAPE

My savage heart

Sleeps in thorn thickets

In a sweet-smelling savanna

Where spiky passions

Drip blue salt

On restless rocks

That patina time

Under a white moon

That reflects

Deep caverns

Of soft tongues

That travel kiss by kiss

Over nocturnal skin

AMAGANSSET BEACH SONG

Seagulls glide above the spray

nest in thighs of white birch,

chorus to a bright yellow moon.

A chipped pitcher of pink peonies

paint a still-life on the table,

breeze-ruffled lace curtains

pool beneath the open window

where starlight spatters the pine floor

and an old marmalade cat snores,

her fur a ripple of dreams.

I shed my clothes and walk down

the dimly lit hallway, knowing

I'll find you asleep in the four-poster.

I lie down beside you, listen to night

whisper in the soft summer sand.

SUMMER VACATION

White froth rides the shoulders
of the endlessly surging sea

casting its lathered treasures
on the patiently waiting shore

while seagull's scalloped wings
beat against the cloud-dappled sky.

Oh, to lie on the soft warm sand
dream beneath a rippling palm,

inhale the smells of salt and brine,
count stars in the green summer.

NEW YORK STORY

The room smelled like spring –
crimson roses, pink peonies,
white orchids and babies' breath.

Ornate iron railings separated
seating groups under mellow light
shimmering through stained-glass windows.

White linen cloths with floral centerpieces,
starched crisp napkins, silver service,
and crystal glasses on slender stems.

He looked tanned and handsome, his smile
reaching his eyes, one blue, the other
hazel . . . always an unexpected surprise.

He ordered wine, they toasted one another,
made small talk as they ate oysters,
green salad and fillets of beef.

When their favorite chocolate dessert came
he told her he was getting married next week,
didn't want her to hear through the 'grapevine'.

On Third Avenue, in front of the restaurant,
they embraced, walked in opposite directions.
"Sign Of The Dove" is no longer in business.

ONCE UPON A TIME

In those halcyon days and inflamed nights

summer danced in throbbing veins

on dewy boughs heavy with fruit.

Our laughter chimed in the steamy air

as searing sun blushed our winter skin.

We left sandy footprints on beach shadows,

dipped our toes into the tide –

our smiles brightly colored, like sea-glass . . .

once upon a time.

NO MESSAGE

Our bodies are turned away in sleep,
opposite poles on rumpled sheets

Was it gentle songs or muffled words,
sentences garbled in sand, or old notes

siphoned through holes in an hourglass,
alphabet scraps on pieces of parchment

fleshing out that tired story, paragraphs
of our latest and greatest lament.

Was it too much to expect—to be in sync
with the sun? Now we watch its sphere
vanish, weightless into an insipid sea

leaving a message of no message.

PAINTED LADIES

In a twilight of butterflies,
jeweled wings sparkle at dusk
reflected on the mirrored pond
in waning summer light.

Painted Ladies, bodices ruffling,
sip marigold and milkweed,
but soon their white powder thins.

You and I, new and soaring
come together as folded wings,
powder barely smudged.

* *Painted Lady butterflies do not live long.*
Commonly found in California, they are
not in danger of extinction.

THE TIME OF YOU AND ME

In the time of you and me, we lived

by the blue and boisterous sea

where exuberant waves roiled

beneath voluptuous skies,

blushed pink and gold at sunset.

The moon and sun conspired

and we fell into a starry abyss,

swam on currents of warm flesh,

in the forgetfulness of a kiss.

REGRETS

rain whispers

wet endearments

to a faded photograph

where two hearts

repeated love words

from watered mouths.

now prostrate I bow low

like the willow –

touch the earth

and pray for your return.

WEEKENDS AT THE BEACH

We caught fifty-two blues on the fishing trip-
pulled into dock, watched the crew clean them.

You got the ice bin from the car.
While waiting I sold three fish, $5 each.
Returning, you said we could be fined.
"I didn't know," was my huffy reply.

On the way to the beach house we stopped
at Captain Jacks, sold most of the fish,
bought some salmon and tuna for sushi
and two huge lobsters.

You put them on the back seat and drove off.
We made faces at each other as they clawed
in the paper bag.

"I'm not putting those things in a pot."
You said you would.
"I'll be in charge of sushi."

I never made sushi before. How hard could it be?
Roll the sticky rice, put that black seaweed stuff on,
lay the salmon or tuna on top.

Continued...

At home we showered and found the lobster pot.
I took my stuff and spread it out on the dining table.
When the rice was done I shaped it into little logs.
Damn that stuff, half of it got under my fingernails.

In a while you asked for the lobsters. I pointed downward.
"Are you crazy - why are they on the floor?'
"I'm racing them, but they won't go in the same direction,
so I don't know whose winning."

You started to laugh...and I started laughing,
and we laughed and laughed until we fell down
next to the befuddled lobsters,
and somehow we ended up in the bedroom.

Three days later when I changed the sheets
I was still picking grains of rice from the bed and floor.

THE GEOGRAPHY OF YOU

Dawn's thin light reveals an island

of flesh asleep on blue sheets.

Symmetry of muscle and bone,

vulnerability in crook of spine

half-hidden in night shade.

Fingers tread over pulsing tributaries,

stretches of moist morning skin,

and my lips, my lips speak in tears,

lamenting the moon's pull, sea sounds

recalling melodies of salty winds

that anchor you to stars in strange lands.

TO MORNING

Under a moonlit canopy
hung in a purpled sky

Naked as peeled plums
we lie dreaming

Night scents disappear
on morning's perfumed air

And like shooting stars
we ride shafts of light

white moths to morning.

TUSCANY DAYDREAM

Blue shutters on kitchen windows
frame trees bursting with blooms.
Birds teeter on mossy boughs,
chatter in Italian bird-talk;

Ivy curls on the stucco walls,
a chipped table, two rusted chairs
on the pebble-strewn patio.

In the abundant vegetable garden
asparagus and artichoke for supper.
For supper some lamb, maybe poultry,
a wedge of cheese, ripe red berries.

I'll bathe in the antique porcelain tub,
dab perfume behind my ears,
wear the cameo you gave me,
and slip into the flowered silk dress.

Down in the musty cellar, I'll open red wine –
let it breathe, take Mama's crystal goblets
from the old bleached pine cupboard.

In the courtyard I inhale sweet air,
listen to the cherub-carved gate creak
and watch the moonlight whiten your shirt,
turn your teeth to pearl . . .

walk into your arms.

TWENTY FOUR HOURS

In morning's petaled air
the willows greenly sway

In afternoon's heated breath
grasses weave a silken thread

In the vestiges of sundown
twilight nods its heavy head

In pillowed night clouds
blue mountains touch the sky

And at the hour before dawn
beneath the moons shadowed face

Dew laden roses stretch and unfurl
as I do . . . for you

READING RAPUNZEL

"Rapunzel, Rapunzel, let down your hair"

It was not unintended, sleepy-eyed babes barely listening,
when I chose *Rapunzel* as a bedtime story.

It was not accidental that I was more enchanted than they,
charmed by the handsome prince and happy ending.

I read on . . .

comforted by those sleep-filled eyes, shutting out day,
dreaming their baby dreams.

So why not, in dim half-light, should I not have mine,
I too, hoped for happily-ever-after.

Now, children are grown with children of their own,
read stories and have dreams of their own.

As for mine . . . well,

I'm fine, but sometimes when wind stirs the breeze
and new buds burst forth, or I see a white carousel horse -
more than anything, I want to let my hair down.

WHITE PEACHES

Scents of morning
quicken leaf breath

mount clouds
waft into gardens

dispel the smell
of night play

midnight musk
daylight dew

sweet sap
white peaches

and you and you and you

WILL YOU STILL LOVE ME

when autumn slips into winter chill
and daybreak glints green leaves bronze
before they tumble into twilight

when you see my breath on white air
and birds spread their wings and flee
leaving empty notes warbling there

when tides are swallowed by the sand
and the blue sea sweeps my scent away
blurring time and fading memory

when wind blows its cold white quiver
and forges ice into cracked rivers
will you regard my lined reflection
past all time and fast fleeting seasons
will you still love me . . .
when the moon turns blue

THE BELLS

The clock strikes time to silence.

I fall into darkness,

lost in the uprooted debris of old lamentations.

I cling to your body,

rest in the sweet dust of your breath,

inhale sacraments of roses and wine.

Somewhere beyond tears I can hear the bells

ringing their mournful rhythm

into my bloodless heart

and the murmur of wind or weeping.

SUMMER-WINTER ROMANCE

Love arrives disguised in unexpected packages

a tender smile across a well-worn face

attraction beyond time, ageless as desire

My head said no . . . my heart shouted stay,

so eagerly, joyfully, I kissed the years away.

SUMMER'S GONE

As pale as the parched roses
parted from sun and dew,
time has torn you from my lips,
and I, the summer of your heart,
am not a wintry thing.

You ask me to forsake the clock,
be faithful to a vow, desire you
as when you were my hungers
perfect meal, ambrosia to my thirst.

Charms fade as do the seasons,
the loveliest of lies are broken oaths –
and tongues, hot palms and pulsing blood
have come to a cold hush.

Though love's not blind, it sees through
a myopic eye and reveals a fallow garden
now that the heat of August is gone.

CADENCE

Slivers of night light
bleach white sheets

Stars swallow sounds
silence seizes breath

Shadows on the wall
play on moonbeams

A labyrinth of limbs
in a four poster bed

REBIRTH

Spring unlooses green
slakes the river's drought

Assuages wheat hills
arouses unripe fruit

Roses thread through
unflowered seasons

Uncovering the dust
of old kisses.

ONE SHORT SEASON

Nightime and sleep bring little relief –
listening to the rain unrelentingly weep.

Snow doesn't soften the mountainside,
trails of grisly thistle are underneath,
and beds of wild roses still have thorns.

Listen to the sound of a train whistle . . .
it can break your heart, like a lover's
betrayal stealing off in the fog, and morning
remembers only the grief.

It resides in every room, in each corner
where no fire can warm, and mute tears
howl like wolves in locked chambers,

where the flame once warm is now cold,
and the ache too big to be contained
in one small summer, in one short season –

too hot, too brief.

NO MAN IS AN ISLAND

Light through mullioned windows
casts waves on blue walls.

A robin perched on a naked branch
warbles his morning aria.

You sleep sprawled across my bed,
an island on white sheets.
Unhurried, I skim hills and valleys
garbed in damp rosy flesh.

Awakening slowly you reach out,
steal over me like sunlight.

DAY TO NIGHT

Evening drops its dusky aftermath

soft as the spread of a thousand stars

yielding to the elusive moon

tucked into a cliff of clouds, while crickets

rub their legs together making melodies

in the wet grass, a lullaby singing us to sleep

so we can dream the dream of lovers

until a kiss summons the morning.

MEMORIES

No moon or stars tonight,
only memories to shed light
through the empty spaces
between raw raindrops.

Just enough to fill a hole
in the shallows of my heart;
and rain falling, falling,
drowning the dreams, fragile,
ethereal as starlight –

threads of hope, trembling fingers
pulling you back again.

MEDITERRANEAN SUNSET

A thousand seagulls explode in the sky,

into mist that shudders and shifts

the new moon imprinting

its golden patina on wavelets

lapping harmoniously adrift – seductive

as the first moments of being in love.

Schools of small dolphin fly from the sea,

wave farewell on each gentle crest.

In the white wake the village recedes,

its peaked orange roofs reclaimed by night

like a lover's arms welcoming the beloved.

In another sun-flushed port we make vows,

until, like last night's waning moon,

they are swallowed by a complacent sea.

AFTERTASTE OF BLISS

A thrusting sea exposes secrets

with each subtle stroke

where the surf pounds and hisses

whirlpools of desire

in the dim eddy of a dream,

and your kiss . . .

syrupy aftertaste of bliss

breaches spume-crested waves,

burgeoning and breathtaking.

LOVERS

The hush of morning

wakes a brilliant sky,

high on sunshine.

We close our eyes,

stretch and fly, breeze-stroked.

Two shooting stars plunging

into a slow river

where our cries shake the earth.

LATE BLOOM

Spring is like a new romance,

a mirage, a chimera –

maples rouged in red stain,

a night sky shot with stars,

flowers, impossible vanity –

cultivated yearning, significant

only in its ending when beauty dims

and possession loosens its grip,

allowing the bud of real love to bloom.

WHEN MORNING COMES

Under the moon's cold white eye

the creek runs silver with winter.

Barren trees bend under a vacant sky

and a solitary bird lifts to the light.

My dreams are singular tonight

without complex variations,

content to lie in your arms

until tomorrow, when anticipation

fails to meet expectation.

LAMENT

In an hourglass of old notes,

sand muffles off-key songs

of our latest lament –

not in tune with the sinking sun,

its orange ball stirs the sea

until night paints a face in the sky –

and what's beautiful becomes empty;

cotton clouds scurry for cover

and we, across a wave of white sheets,

our arms reaching out in sleep

are lost in memories we can't retrieve.

DANCING ON THE EDGE

Our mouths
speak in tongues

raw words
undigested

dancing on the edge
precarious

like a rush of water
downstream

tumbling over rocks
with deaf ears

COUNTING THE STARS

The sun slips into the water

bequeaths night her golden rays

swelling reflections on a glistening bay.

Two suns at once, above and below.

The wanton moon rises

spreading soft butter light

as incandescent stars glow

halfway between day and night.

CELLAR DOOR

We lift the cellar door . . .

light seeps into crevices,
down narrow stone steps
varnished dust
of yesterdays

We pause . . .

light illuminates bushels of rotting apples
flowers strung upside down, drying dying
a tattered old quilt,
a mouse skeleton whiskers intact
a lacquered box on a rickety table
a sepia photograph
a man and woman smiling
coffee stained paper
bond mark 1903
an unfinished love poem

Someone told us . . .

"cellar door" was the prettiest phrase
mold fills our nostrils
We dash up the stairs
into the sunlight
anxious to create
our own memories

MY DREAM

In the stillness of water

infused with streams of sleep

and the infinite blurring of blue –

swirling, constant, soundless

as limbs fluttering on distant shores

where morning doves chatter in the space

between darkness and dawn.

A SNOWSTORM REMEMBERED

Gauze curtains billow above the bed.
I breath deep your sweet smell of sleep –
snow lilies fragrant on soft white sheets.

Barefoot and blanketed, I go to the door,
gaze at the frigid rime-ceilinged sky,
watch as six-sided crystals shower
the tawny grass with glistening flakes.

Fine powder coats the holly's red berries,
frosted pines are decorated with icicles.
Vapid memories, wedding cake white
drip confections like sodden kisses
into spidery cracks on the frozen stream.

Wisps of air catch in my throat, my breath
makes smoke circles that vanish on my cheek,
melt away like snow, and I in my great conceit,
let you go.

PAST PRIME

Autumn leaves past prime,
colors subdued,
whisper secrets of seasons
layered with veils of leaves.

Promise one more season,
one more flowering,
one more autumn,
past prime.

AND I REMEMBER

The lake is shadowed, veiled with images,
reflections of a mystic moon, the silken rustlings
of wind-stirred violets, and I remember . . .

flower-scented meadows ringed with tall trees,
long-beaked birds thrusting themselves
into the sun's yellow eye, and I remember . . .

smoothing a blue blanket under the chestnut,
holding hands as we settled into soft earth
inhaling warm breath, and I remember . . .

sweet strawberries and cool wine, your lips
on my tongue tasting the sugary red juice
as if it were your own, and I remember . . .

at midnight, through my bedroom window
the lake looked so still, and the moon pale,
without color, when I remember . . .

FALLING IN LOVE WITH OCTOBER

I have fallen in love with October again,
red and gold leaves whispering in pristine air.

I have fallen in love with October again,
the breeze whishing overhead, soft as a hymn.

I have fallen in love with October again,
pink-cheeked children romping in the leaves,
their bodies warm as new mittens.

I have fallen in love with October again,
the cloudless blue sky and the tumbling leaves
rushing . . . rushing toward winter.

SEA-GLASS MEMORIES

On the shore waves whisper

sandy secrets that linger

like laughter on the languid air.

Sun blushes our winter skin,

our shadows stripe the beach,

imprint images that capture

the moment, tucked carefully away

like sea-glass, polished by time.

WITHOUT DAWN

No love amongst the dead –
they wear shrouds, waltz with dust,
the sea drinks their tears

while a chaste yellow moon
beams on the rock-strewn shore
where light collides with night.

A star-studded sky smolders
in the water's tarnished mirror,
reflects a drop of blood
on the moon's rutted face.

Once pure shape, now spirit,
never to be soothed again
by daylight's white cheek.

The ocean's moribund depths
inhale the bitter breathe
replete with bones and ashes.

No love amongst the dead –
they wear shrouds, waltz with dust,
the sea drinks their tears,

and love without dawn is nothing at all.

AND SO TO DREAM . . .

Wind unlatches the shadowed gate,

moonlight spills white on dim walls.

I hold solitary vigil in a hushed house,

balance precariously on the ledge

of sleep and wakefulness.

Muffled voices in undefined space,

illusive acuity beyond awareness,

hovering between dream and reality.

The clock ticks minutes to morning

marking acquaintance with mortality.

I shut out the night sounds –

the cicadas' hum, an owl's muted hoot,

the gate swinging slowly . . .

THE OTHER SIDE OF THE SUN

Sleep-filled clouds shift,
silence the cries of seagulls
paying homage to night's corona.

In the depth of star-filled fields
spiky coral bleeds her secrets
into the heavy heart of time.

On the other side of the sun
yellow-robed sunflowers turn
as they fold into gold-green sleep.

Night pulls her shadowed shawl
over tree branches that swing
like cradles hung from the moon.

DOWNPOUR

Sudden rain bleeds through
red rays of waning winter sun,
splashes on the brittle earth
and spins its deep deluge
from the gray gaze of sky.

On the forest's sculpted floor
the sluggish smell of spruce
expels its pungent green breath
over the wet crisscrossing roots.

It rumbles on the rooftop, weeps
down the windowpanes, and glitters
like a thousand stars if you narrow
your eyes and squint.

LOVE'S LABOR

The sun makes its slow descent,
obliterating yet another afternoon.

In a basin of warm soapy water
I wash my mother's feet.

She curls her toes, grimaces,
retreats from the bubbles.

I think she stares at a fleck of light
sparkling on the window glass,

maybe her own vanishing reflection.

SNAPSHOTS OF MY FATHER

When I was six I learned to swim across the lake.
My father would paddle the row boat, and I swam
alongside to the other shore, and back again.

I thought the sun magically turned his sandy hair
and mustache gold.

When I was nine he took me to watch handball
in the park. "No betting," my mother said.

We walked side by side and held hands.
When I gazed up at him he smiled. I felt proud --
he was so handsome in the white cable-knit sweater
my mother had made.

He did bet two dollars on the handball game . . .
but I never told.

NEW MOON

Tides of the new moon

pool and lap on salt mud-flats

where the sea has fled from

sand-dollars and scallop-backed shells

whimpering under the weight

of flamingo and scarlet ibis,

I hurry under the cover of darkness

to the comforting arms of home.

NIGHT TIME

Draped in night's dark light
free from the weight of flesh

Veiled murmurs stroke my ear
muffle even the deep silence

And thoughts that slowly disappear like smoke
dispelling cares of the day

In my isolated evening lair I am kissed
by the mouth of a placid moon

Swaddled and cradled, a babe in watery arms
as I am delivered into a dream

NIRVANA

To fly like an eagle,

wings swishing on wind's whim

their clouded flight

over mirrored seas

beneath orange sunsets

in the hum of stars

listening

to the stunning music of water

BLUE HEAVEN

The summer cottage

hosts a garden

where flowers unfurl

under cotton-clad skies.

Toss your shoes to the wind

dip your toes into dark earth

slip into the polished quiet of dusk

drink sweet tea from eggshell cups

eat a piece of dew-dipped fruit

salivate with anticipation

for an unopened book

DESIRE LINES

Maybe the lines on a tree or rings
around an elephant's trunk
don't define their age, but are desire lines.

Maybe every line is a wish,
a dream unfulfilled, a longing.

Maybe the lines on our faces
are secret desires –
experiences not had, a road untaken,
a love not embraced.

Would you erase those lines, that history?
Or would you navigate the same journey,
take the same road again?

Take an inventory, check your desire lines . . .
be careful what you decide.

MORNING GIFTS

A small pale green tree-frog
sits on a leaf still wet with night,
his chest puffs and deflates
waiting for sunshine to dry
the last dewdrops on his back.

Flaming monarch butterfly rides
on spirals of fresh sweet air,
the hummingbird beats his wings
a thousand times for one perfumed sip
of a succulent pink peony.

If you stand very still in the garden
morning will untie her colorful ribbons –
unwrap her generous gifts.

NIGHT SOLACE

Between transitory tears
Shreds of voices shift
Drop by drop.

Sweet night spirit me to sleep
Let me crawl into your skin
Become my dream.

Hold tight, hold back the light
Hold back the morning.

THE PEONY

Her green stem prods yielding soil,
sprouts leafy arms and grows tall.

Pink and perfect, proudly bloomed,
she embraces summer's wanton play
while a hundred ants have their way.

Her plummy heart honeys the air
with sweetness to pacify angry gods
who cannot abide such perfection.

REKINDLED

The slowly running creek, almost still,
weeps beneath the moon's vacant eye.

An owl swivels on a leafless limb,
hoots disdain to the vast cold sky.

Purple smoke whorls in the chimney,
whispers across a crusted plain.

In the window candlelight sputters
on a woman's black satin gown.

Silvered hair smartly plaited,
ruby earrings swing against her neck.

Blue-veined hands finger the mantle
desirous of the hearth's hot flame.

Sparks rekindled from scorched ashes
flushes her skin with old desire

when fire was not the only source of heat.

RISING TIDE

Our restless hearts thrum

to the sea's ageless surge.

We swim in nocturnal waters

under the ripe red moon.

Sand, seaweed, and mud marry,

render our blood senseless,

stroke through our veins

until only the spray remains.

SEAGULLS

Wings spread

white banners in flight

silver-tipped feathers

beacons of light

diving soaring

like hungry dogs

rummaging through

the last scraps of debris

starved as the foam

that eats the sand

TANGLED WEBS

Ivy spreads its green tentacles
strangles the daisies and roses –
an unnoticed smothering.

I glided easily into your arms,
easy as a spider slides down
strands of bright sunlight,

sure that our love would grow
slowly and strong enough
to complete the journey,

but roads turn, even crumble,
and we were hardly able to breath
through a another summer day.

A CENTRAL PARK KIND OF MORNING

Early sun shimmies across the eastern sky,
brightens the city's dark shadowy hush.

The homeless sleep on harsh stone pillows
or slatted benches under nodding trees.

Strays rummage through empty trash bins
eternally hopeful of some meager treat.

Golden sunlight strokes the cool grass warm,
coaxes tight-fisted buds into bloom

Sleepy songbirds untuck tiny ruffled heads,
lazily stretch perfectly pleated wings.

In our own sky-high aerie, I reach for you
across the white rumpled sheets,

anticipate the sunrise swell, pink and slow –
revealing you . . . and a new morning.

WALK ON THE HEART SIDE

Come walk with me love . . .
let's walk on the heart side

take my hand, let our fingers
entwine, weave intimacies

before love, while my breasts
are generous with longing

before your smoldering flame
eclipses the shadows on the moon

and starlight spills on my pale skin
diaphanous as a daydream

Come walk with me love . . .
let's walk on the heart side.

Breinigsville, PA USA
26 November 2010
250016BV00001B/7/P

FEB - - 2012